The Cards Don't Lie: Wisdom, Strength and Honesty

Kimberly Cooney

BookLeaf Publishing

India | USA | UK

Presentation by BookLeaf Publishing
Web: www.bookleafpub.com
E-mail: info@bookleafpub.com

ISBN: 978-93-5744-993-9
First edition 2022

DEDICATION

Buddy Boy,

I hope you can be proud of who I've grown up to be.

I miss you.

ACKNOWLEDGEMENT

To my mom - for reading all my story assignments for school over the years and thinking "Wow! my kid can write like this?"
 I love you Lady

To Munchkin & Munchkinette - Auntie Kimmy wants you both to know she loves you and believes you each can be great at whatever you choose.

To Amanda Lovelace - you inspire me and I'm sure many others with your gift for writing. Thank you and please keep creating.
And shout-out to Janaina Mediros for the beautiful artwork of the oracle deck.

To all who have decided to be my readers - thank you for supporting the dream of a young woman. Please enjoy and spread the word of my book; it would mean the world to me.

PREFACE

Inspired by the "believe in your own magic" oracle deck by best-selling poet Amanda Lovelace, I have created a poem-a-day based on the oracle card I had drawn.

Each day I asked "what will today's poem focus on?" as I shuffled the deck and cleared my mind. Once a card was drawn, I referred to the guide Amanda Lovelace wrote to accompany the cards and I interpreted the meaning to create my poems.

Confidence

time, practice,
evolution.

you must break down your cage to enjoy the
freedom beyond.

unlearn the toxic ideals thrust upon you
and bloom into the desert rose inside.

slay your fears and let your spark burn.

Garden

care for thy self;
don't let pain or failure,
fear or the dirty words of others
stifle you.

raise your face to the glorious sun,
bask and revel in your inner strength,
then the true you that deserves to blossom
will sprout.

Grey

the only thing for certain is inevitability.

endings happen, pain happens but
so do beginnings and healing.

look for the grey; the possibility
in a world of black and white.

Sword

change is all around –
it is in the air, in the earth, in our blood.

we can consider all the outcomes;
fear what may happen
but change comes whether we want it to or
not.

so embrace this revolution;
slay those fears and doubts,
and wield your strength and perseverance
as your greatest weapon.

Clover

guilt smothers your fire;
guilt weighs you down.

you must choose your path:
    let guilt rule you
            or
    push ahead in your life.

there is no correct answer but sometimes
that is the answer you need.

Tower

relax...   unplug...

ideals like these become more difficult each
day - each hour – each second,
but don't let life's toils take control of you.

self-love and self-care are the best
medicine.

recharge and
rediscover

yourself.

Potion

self-love:
be kind to your body and mind;
care for your palace.

through loving thy self and nurturing your
soul your physical and mental health need
that attention now

more than the worries about tomorrow.

Sun

don't be that person
   - that circles a lover.

create your own happiness instead.

don't let others have the power to bring you
joy;
for you deserve to be happy
without others dictating your feelings.

brighten your own sky; light your own way.

Raindrops

take a chance.

though you've been mistreated and left out
in the cold before,
don't let that stop you from enjoying the
world in all its beauty.

stomp on their misconceptions like a puddle
under your feet
and soak in the drizzle of new possibilities.

Voyage

in truth,
you have all the answers.

stop looking outside, for the approval of
others and instead
focus on looking inside yourself;

be your own guide.

enjoy the journey to find your destination.

Castle

burning bridges is easy -
moving forward is harder.

emotions can get the best of us
and force you to make decisions we never
realized needed to be made.

healing will follow with intuition as your
compass.

step forward through the ashes of the past
and
don't look back.

Spaceship

sing loud and use your voice;
force others to really hear you.

be the boss:
don't let others silence you;
don't let them talk for you,
over you
or interrupt you.

your voice can move mountains,
make waves,
turn tides.

make them hear your roar!

Shark

the prettiest things are ugliest on the inside.

people break each others' hearts
but they cannot truly break your spirit.

leave toxicity behind and
lead with your inner strength.

despite what the masses believe,
it is ok to be independent.

Lighthouse

your all is always enough.

show self-love, self-kindness,
self-confidence and

stand strong because you can.

speak out because you can.

make others hear you because you can.

be your own hero and
 most importantly
   just be you.

Storm

things will get better;
a rainbow will come after the storm.

you are strong enough
to make it through and

you will be better on the other side.

Evil Queen

toxic people poison you and
they need to be exiled from your life.

second chances have no time for no good
people and
you have a clear path ahead of you.

so don't let evil queens hold you back;

be the true queen you were meant to be.

Witch

karma is a witch.

good deeds bring good vibes but
wrong doings cause suffering.

be a good witch and let come what may.
justice comes to all.

I'll get mine   and
   you'll all get yours.

Lavender

share the best version of you with those
who love and support that side of you.

find your tribe and
trust that they care for you.

listen to their advice but do decide for
yourself;
they will encourage you no matter your
choice.

Red

forgiveness is not an obligation.

follow your own terms
 and consider if enough time has passed to
do what you must.
grudges can hold you back
but you can push on.

let the light of forgiveness draw you toward
moving on to a better place in your life.

Nostalgia

we all wish past moments could have been different but this daydreaming of "what if" is interfering with your present.

learn from the former but the now is what's happening.

grow and enjoy what is right in front of you instead of wanting to better something you have
no way of changing.

for what's done is done.

Thornes

share the love by
being the support someone needs.
help others bloom and dust off their crowns.

show the care once given to you that guided
you to your crown;
that helped you polish it
and own it.

help someone else find their shine.